EVEN WITH CLIMATE CHANGE HAIKU

the days are still flush
with shivering spring again
the days go cooly

STUPID ME HAIKU

i stumble these days
wait stupidly to die here
happy i am now

UNLUCKY SPRING HAIKU

the days pass from dawn
till the music of nighttime
i hum poems waiting

THE MARROW BLEEDS TO SEED HAIKU

waking slowly now
a third time in the morning
over a cup of brew

SPRING LULLABY HAIKU

the days warn slowly
even now from chill to heat
the porch is stunning

MARCH 25TH HAIKU

the warm sunlight creeps
through morning portals it flows
to the forest floor

LOVE AND NATURE

these broken twigs show
the rustic signs of my heart
...my love is wooded

COUNTRY GIRL HAIKU

you are sweetest song
heart of the farm and forest
for you i live, die

SPRING SINGS SILLY HAIKU

hear the water lap
the shores of the melted lake
....with only kisses

BRSK LOGIC HAIKU

one step at a time
toward where the bottom leads to
at the end of it

BRISK NONSENSE HAIKU

walk rapidly nowhere
on nothingness crazy sore
with memories gone

SPRING SHIVERS HAIKU

early dawn we wake
the sunlight creeps upon us
outside the porch door

WINDMILLS HAIKU

windmills make movement
for power from the ocean
far out in the waves

THE PROBLEM HAIKU

i was born wrongly
some part of me was dumb then
...unable to speak

WHAT STRANGE THING HAIKU

what strange thing was it?
that caused my collapse these years
...strange thing forgotten

I AM HAPPY HAIKU

i am happy now
live well with my confusion
in this strange country

THE TRAGIC HEART LAUGHS HAIKU

here in old age laugh
like us god laughs just as well
all night by the fire

EACH BLADE OF GRASS HAIKU

life and death in each
in each stringy blade of grass
...stand up and laugh now

JOY HAIKU

music and nature
fill the world the trees, oceans
flood my heart with love

DESCENT HAIKU

down we went enjoined
to the basement of our love
to stare at ourselves

FRONTAL LABOTOMY HAIKU

as i age dull mind
i grow pacific inside
...waddle in the sun

WE SMILE ACHING HAIKU

laughter falls upon us
with our pain...is part of age
this way of our lives

PUSHING LIKE NAKED SPRING HAIKU

root to bud this time
innocent and stubbornly
i fallow downward

THE STUPID WAYS WE LOVE HAIKU

simple and singular
dully straight toward your heart
i give you my gift

STILL SHIVERIG HAIKU

winter keeps a cold
eye on the paths that i take
blows to let me know

SEEDS HAIKU

they are put away
in the soil and forgotten
until fall darkens

AFTERNOON HAIKU

the hot buttery
sunlight of a late mid-spring day
made me so sleepy

APRIL IS A CURSE HAIKU

april is a curse
made to crucify small gods
..weak, they drown always

NAKED REMNANTS HAIKU

not from the bath but
from winter's trees clawing out
the earth in springtime

STEWING HAIKU

only music calms
in this cycle of pure nerves
no cigarettes now

DAYS OF WONDERFUL NOTHIING HAIKU

nothing happens now
...this day yawns and streches out
like a fat balloon

OLD CAT HAIKU

i am confronted
the whole mad swirl of everything to come begins now!

  What's New
  Poetry Forum
  Short Stories
  Mad Gallery
  Open Mic
  Submissions

Sam Silva

Three Haiku: Sale, Lucky, Gnats
featured in the poetry forum October 21, 2021 :: 0 comments

THE SALE

this huge house I love
...this relic of a small past
...away and gone now

***
LUCKY GUY

I was luckiest
when things fell apart. The world
baked like dough to bread

***
GNATS

gnats swarm in the sun
the day is itchy rotten
the apple stinks too much
editors note:

Just as life comes in short bursts; our luck can turn on the sale of a gnat. – mh clay
LIGHT HAIKU
featured in the poetry forum July 19, 2021 :: 0 comments

a light diffuses black
..it lathers the sky that way
...clouds spread like thunder
editors note:

A light lather is a close shave. – mh clay

FRANKENSTEIN
featured in the poetry forum April 30, 2021 :: 0 comments

Places where the dead are plugged
...electric to all passion's core
wandering the peasant groves
...confused by an uncertain brain
and terrorizing man and beast
and women also
like a boar
searching warmth
in fear of fire.
Destruction in desire's feast
the way the dead can feel desire!!
editors note:

Like this, we grope our grove, in search of life's bright bolt. – mh clay

LIVING AMONG THE MIDDLE CLASSES
featured in the poetry forum February 2, 2021 :: 0 comments

An achy nervousness
among pandemic days
while summer turns toward Fall
and the politics of madness
in the election of it all

and my own old age decays
dully for its sadness
like some disease which slays

with a sleep that fills our eyes
with an image on TV
of dreamy dreamy hot fires
in the skies.
editors note:

Flat screen, flat deal! We are what we watch. – mh clay

THE LOVE BOND
featured in the poetry forum November 7, 2020 :: 0 comments

See we are ancient already! We are marble
carved and sealed to fortressed stone
inseparable the way we aged together
and glistening in our polish
like one of your starry paintings.

Or an old rustic house
grown out as one toward the woodland.
We live in the same skin
shelter under each other's locks.

I look out the window of your brilliant eyes
and see and give utterance for the world
eternally brand new!
editors note:

Yes! Give utterance! – mh clay

FAILED ARTIST
featured in the poetry forum August 17, 2020 :: 0 comments

Nature's first rule is predation
a fact in the face
which he could not stand

so he puffed up a cloud
in his glacial station
to obscure that cruel beauty
of the land.
editors note:

In this case, smoke 'em when you DON'T… – mh clay

ART AS THE GHOSTLY SOPRANO
featured in the poetry forum June 15, 2020 :: 0 comments

This is the love among the dead
…these are those high operatic notes
…that gorge of meat and wine and bread
…that private castle leaking hope, despair,
the two the same in desperate sighs

encased in predatory motes
to keep away the warlike herds
of Mongols milking mares and goats
with lost dreams much like lullabies
composed by angels

….without words…
editors note:

And, yet, we must sing them… – mh clay

THE MUSIC OF THE OCEAN'S COAST
featured in the poetry forum April 10, 2020 :: 0 comments

Midnight longing for God and Heaven
Horns of sweet jazz for Jesus
in the missionary night.

Converting bats like me to bliss,
bugs, to that kiss of divinity
...the lucky and beloved to a sigh
alike the sea
editors note:

Sing contentment in every key. – mh clay

A CITY LIKE BERLIN
featured in the poetry forum January 20, 2020 :: 0 comments

Fire at night! Fire
in the coal dark cold
of an ice like desire
that chokes the eyes
like wicked smoke
under shrouded skies
and bilious smog

…and a breathy toke
on a deadly drug
which sells the soul
which howls like a dog
in lightning storms
against thunder sounds
whose big guns bellow a hundred rounds
on our crumbling station
our crumbling forms
our tired nation
our hell-bent choir.

Fire at night….such wicked fire!
editors note:

Public works or public outrage? What's happening in your city? – mh clay

TIRED MEN OF THE ASHES
featured in the poetry forum November 4, 2019 :: 0 comments

The manifest of my dreams
in spring
is written cool, bland,
lyrically lazy
about the green shrubbery
and the yellow brown roses
come ugly upon a trailer park Easter

...a bit of leafy stem
sticks its head above
the loam

and this is our Jesus!, our poetry!
editors note:

Jesus in every flower. Resurrection in every Spring. – mh clay

1
2
3
?

magazines. He was nominated a total of seven times by three small presses and has a full length collection of poetry called Eating and Drinking based on a royalties contract signed with Bright Spark Creative available for order at any online bookstore and has other full length poetry books available at amazon.com. Three spoken word CDs of Sam Silva's have been marketed through CDBaby.

What's New
Poetry
Short Stories
Mad Gallery
Open Mic
Submissions
Merch
Contact

© 2021
...a cat each time we argue
...old and tired...lumpy

WHOLE HEART HAIKU

I am your grin now
...what you laugh at knowingly
your eyes sparkling up

ENORMOUS PROBLEM HAIKU

stuck on it to sleep
and deaming the wrong things too
always late at night

STUPID RULES HAIKU

keep me from dreaming
and give me nightmares as well
much as i try not